ABTAPL GUIDE

FOR

THEOLOGICAL

LIBRARIES

Michael Gale and Carol Reekie

ABTAPL Publishing

Compiled and edited under the auspices of ABTAPL, the
Association of British Theological and Philosophical Libraries.

www.abtapl.org.uk

ABTAPL was formed in 1956 to promote the cause of
librarianship in these special fields and to disseminate
information about techniques, collections and
publications relevant to its members.

For further information about the Association, please contact:

www.abtapl.org.uk   or

Carol Reekie
Cambridge Theological Federation
Wesley House
Jesus Lane
Cambridge CB5 8BJ

Tel: 01223 741043
E-mail: cr248@cam.ac.uk

Copyright © 2008   ABTAPL, the Association of
British Theological and Philosophical Libraries.

British Library Cataloguing in Publication Data
A catalogue record for this book available from the British Library

ISBN 978 094894502 1

Printed in Great Britain by Kallkwik, Birmingham.

ii

ABTAPL Guidelines for Theological Libraries

Authorship note

The structure of the text is based on that of the previous edition, authored by Ruth Gibson, Patrick Lambe and Judy Powles, and published as part of a special issue of the ABTAPL *Bulletin* in 1990. The text itself has been substantially rewritten by Michael Gale, librarian of the Queen's Foundation, Birmingham, with the assistance of Carol Reekie, librarian of the Cambridge Theological Federation, and other members of the ABTAPL Committee. It was approved for publication by the ABTAPL Committee at a special meeting on 29th November 2007.

iii

CONTENTS

Abbreviations

ABTAPL :Association of British Theological
And Philosophical Libraries.

ATLA   :American Theological Library
Association.

CILIP   :Chartered Institute of Library and
Information Professionals.

1 INTRODUCTION

1.1 Aims

The purpose of this booklet is to set out guidelines for the provision of library services in colleges involved in theological education and training. It is primarily designed for independent colleges which support courses leading to a formal certificate, diploma or degree. But it is hoped that it will also be of some practical use to the wider range of institutions which constitute the ABTAPL membership.

It also recognises that there is considerable variation in local circumstances, even between colleges which are broadly similar in their scope and objectives. The guidelines should not therefore be regarded as prescriptive. Rather they are intended to offer a broad yardstick to those with responsibility for the provision of library services, taking into account developments both within the library profession and in theological education and training since the publication of the last edition in 1990.

The guidelines are addressed not only to librarians, but also to institutions, and to those with responsibility for their oversight, such as validating universities. This is a key theme of the booklet. Librarians cannot deliver a high quality library service on their own. They need the full support of the institution.

1.2 Developments in librarianship

Perhaps one of the most notable changes in the field of librarianship in the past twenty years has been the redundancy of the term 'librarian'. Although still common within theological libraries, it is now less often used to describe professional posts in the wider higher and further education sectors. Rather, 'information professional', 'knowledge manager', or 'learning resources coordinator' are amongst the terms which are often preferred. One reason for this is that the librarian's job has evolved, or expanded, significantly during this period. In the past librarians were primarily responsible for a physical asset, a 'library', comprising a range of books, journals, audiovisual materials, and possibly some early stand-alone CDROMs. Now it is more common for librarians to be responsible for a more loosely defined 'information service', a library without walls, which may also provide a range of networked or web-based electronic services besides offering support for freely available online resources. The amount of 'information' for which a librarian may be responsible for managing is now limitless.

The concept of information literacy has evolved in parallel with the growing demands of the information society. It is now widely accepted that learning institutions have a generic role to play in helping students to develop lifelong information skills, and librarians have been quick to get involved in this work, building on their traditional role in user education.

In response to these changes, librarians have been required to develop new skills. In particular, they have had to acquire a range of IT skills, for managing automated library systems, training and supporting library users in the use of electronic resources, authoring web pages, and in more general terms operating in a highly automated office environment. But they have also had to develop collaborative skills, as they become more dependent on colleagues with more specific expertise, and advocacy skills, as they seek to challenge traditional perceptions of the library in a less clearly defined institutional environment.

1.3 Developments in theological education and training

The past twenty years have also seen significant changes in theological education and training. The early 1990s saw the consolidation of ordination training provision in fewer institutions. More recently the number of ordinands in full time training has declined sharply, and more flexible, part time, training pathways have been developed to meet the needs of the growing numbers of older candidates. Training budgets have come under closer scrutiny, and the concept of regional partnerships has emerged to make better use of resources[1].

Meanwhile training for lay ministry is expanding, and more independent students are applying for validated programmes. Institutions are diversifying in order to meet the demand. Changing attitudes to mission are impacting on mission training institutions.

For some libraries these changes have brought closure, merger, or relocation. Others have witnessed a significant increase

---

[1] See, for example, Church of England. *Formation for ministry within a learning church: the structure and funding of ordination training* ("The Hind report"). London: Church House Publishing, 2003.

in demand, in particular for off-campus services.

Financial imperatives and a more rigorous quality assurance regime within higher education have seen a trend towards closer ties with local universities. Many theological colleges are now 'affiliated to', or 'in partnership with' a university. Students study on 'validated' or 'collaborative' programmes. For libraries, this raises a variety of questions about access to resources, reciprocal arrangements, and duplication.

1.4 The challenge for theological libraries

For theological libraries, these developments represent both a challenge and an opportunity. Perhaps the biggest challenge is that the financial resources required to support a modern library are greater now than they have ever been, with the escalating cost of traditional materials, additional expenditure on electronic media, and the often hidden costs of maintaining and developing an appropriate IT infrastructure. Theological institutions are often ill-equipped to meet these costs. Many cannot afford full time IT support, and may not recognise the library's IT needs and priorities. Meanwhile many of the electronic resources coming onto the market are beyond the means of small colleges. Institutional pricing tends to be aimed at the university sector with its substantially greater purchasing power. The relative wealth of North American theological libraries also impacts on publishers' pricing strategies. More advocacy is required if theological libraries in the UK are not to be left behind.

The changing profile of library users is also a challenge. Some of the growing numbers of older users may be returning to education after many years' absence, or they may simply be uncomfortable in the modern learning environment. The information skills gap may be considerable. Theological librarians thus have a particularly important role to play in the development of information literacy and training. Furthermore, with a larger and more diverse user base, the service inevitably loses something of its personal touch, which has been one of the traditional strengths of small theological libraries. It also becomes more dependent on systems for its security.

But if the challenges appear great, the opportunities are also considerable. The new technology has hugely expanded the range of resources as well as the modes of delivery which librarians can now offer to their users.

It has also facilitated the collaborative sharing of resources which would have been unthinkable to previous generations. With the appropriate structures in place and a willingness to cooperate on all sides, there is an unprecedented opportunity for resource sharing and cost saving which could greatly benefit smaller institutions.

These developments are the background to the guidelines which follow. The structure of the text is based on the 1990 edition, with major sections on staffing (section 2), collection management (section 3) and library management (section 7). New sections on information technology (section 4) and information literacy (section 5), and a significantly expanded section on library cooperation (section 6) reflect the importance of these topics for a modern theological library. Throughout there is an emphasis on the expanding skills base of the theological librarian and the need for a collaborative approach to the work.

2 STAFFING

The staffing requirements of a theological library will vary according to size, level of use, and the scale of the services provided. But most institutions wishing to provide a modern library service with up-to-date resources now recognise the need for a permanent, full time, professionally qualified librarian with some non-professional support.

2.1 Professional qualification

A professional librarian is required to manage not only the day-to-day operation of the library but also its development in a rapidly changing environment. A professional appointment should therefore be regarded as an investment in what should be the thriving hub of the institution's learning environment.

The routes to a professional qualification are now more flexible following the publication of CILIP's Framework of Qualifications[2]. If a librarian in post wishes to pursue a professional qualification, then the institution should support them.

---

[2] See http://www.cilip.org.uk/qualificationschartership/FrameworkofQualifications/ (accessed 21.9.07)

2.2 Skills

The modern librarian requires a wide range of skills, from traditional skills in management, the organisation of knowledge, and reference work, to the more modern requirement for IT competencies and teaching skills. The ability to work collaboratively, together with the political skills to work effectively within the institution, and a willingness to nurture professional networks in the wider library and educational sectors, are becoming increasingly important. In some institutions the librarian may also be required to fulfil the specialist roles of conservator or archivist. Above all the librarian should be a people person, committed to the ethos of public service and customer care.

But should a theological librarian be a theologian or a church historian? Some subject knowledge is desirable, and some institutions will require the librarian to be in sympathy with the institution's ethos, but a degree in theology or a related subject should not be regarded as a prerequisite. However the institution should support a librarian in post who wishes to enhance their subject knowledge. It is perhaps more important that the librarian is able to work effectively with academic colleagues within the institution and professional colleagues outside it in order to provide an effective service.

2.3 Conditions of employment

The librarian should have a formal contract of employment. The salary should be in accordance with the CILIP salary guide for colleges of higher education[3].

The librarian should be employed throughout the calendar year. Even where library use declines during vacation periods, the work of the librarian goes on. Some tasks, such as stock checking or systems upgrades, are best accomplished during vacations.

2.4 Status

For various reasons librarians have often suffered from a lack of status, with the result that library services do not always receive the support they need from the institution. The library should be at the heart of the mission of a learning institution. Its needs and priorities should be reflected in the

---

[3] See http://www.cilip.org.uk/jobscareers/salaries/salaryguides/hesg.htm (accessed 21.9.07)

institution's priorities and planning, and championed at the highest level.

For this reason the librarian should be responsible directly to the principal (or equivalent), with academic staff status, and membership of the Academic Board. The librarian may also be a member of the IT committee (if there is one) or the teaching committee. This serves to ensure that library services and the teaching curriculum are properly coordinated.

2.5 Authority

The issue of authority can sometimes be a grey area. The librarian is an employee, with a responsibility to the institution, but also a professional, with a wider professional responsibility and code of ethics. The library may also have a remit beyond the members of the institution.

The librarian should have overall responsibility for the day-to-day management of the library, and sufficient authority to carry it out. On issues of policy and development which are of an institutional nature, such as external membership or the future of historic collections, the librarian's professional judgement should be respected. A library mission statement is an important tool for assisting with issues of this nature (see **7.1.1**).

2.6 Library Committee

The librarian should be supported by a Library Committee, which should meet regularly, and act in an advisory and consultative capacity on matters relating to the library. If the Committee is to have a policy-shaping remit, and is to be more than a mere user group (useful though that may be), then it is important that it has sufficient status. For this reason the principal (or a person with appropriate authority) should be a member, along with the librarian, representatives of the academic staff and student body, and an appropriate external person, possibly an external library member and / or a fellow professional librarian.

2.7 Support staff

Some library tasks, such as processing, can be performed just as effectively, and more cheaply, by non-professional support staff. But support staff need to be managed. Their work needs to be planned, supervised – to a greater or lesser extent – and checked. If the balance between professional and support staffing is wrong, then support staff may find themselves with insufficient work to do, simply adding to the pressure on the librarian.

Another issue to consider is whether the library offers self-service (i.e. can users make substantial use of the library in the absence of library staff?). If it does, then there is considerable scope for flexibility over staffing. If it doesn't, then staffing levels – for support staff in particular – must inevitably be linked to opening hours.

2.8 Volunteers

Within theological institutions there tends to be a particularly strong commitment to the institutional community, with a recognition that members can usefully contribute to the effective running of the community in a voluntary capacity. Appropriately trained volunteers can be a big help with tasks such as shelving and stock checking.

But the librarian should also be cautious in recruiting volunteers. Like support staff, they need to be managed, but unlike support staff, there is often no formal commitment or contractual responsibility on the part of the volunteer. Their attendance may be unpredictable. They may leave without notice.

Providing opportunities for voluntary employment in church-related settings is sometimes regarded as a kind way of helping people, but theological librarians should be wary of the costs of providing such opportunities. Volunteers, like paid library staff, should be recruited on merit, and provision should be made for their position to be reviewed on a regular basis.

These formalities also serve to protect volunteers from situations which may not be in their own best interests.

2.9 Professional development

It is in the institution's own interests to further the librarian's professional development. Much can be gained from contacts with other librarians and valuable expertise and knowledge can be acquired from attendance at conferences and courses. This is especially important in small theological libraries where the librarian is likely to be working in professional isolation.

The librarian should be encouraged to attend relevant courses, meetings and conferences organised by professional associations such as CILIP and ABTAPL as part of normal duties. Costs should be covered by the institution's staff training budget.

Visits to other theological libraries should also be encouraged, and regarded as part of the librarian's normal duties. Activities and projects undertaken for an appropriate professional association should also be supported, provided they are relevant to the librarian's work and do not detract from the normal running of the library.

2.10 Appraisal

An annual appraisal (or equivalent) should be seen as a positive, two-way process which benefits both the librarian and the institution. On the one hand it provides an opportunity to reflect on the past year and to set targets for the coming year. But it is also an opportunity to review the way in which the institution supports the librarian, both in terms of its structures (committees, lines of management etc) and in terms of day-to-day working relationships. In this respect, the librarian is likely to occupy a unique position within the institution, and it is important that the appraisal is tailored to reflect the library's particular needs. It may be appropriate, for example, to invite an external person, such as a fellow librarian, to be involved in the process.

The appraisal should also be used to identify training needs, and to support the wider professional development of the librarian. The key to a good appraisal is preparation, and the appraisee should complete an appraisal form prior to the meeting. Afterwards it is important that both parties have a written record of the agreed targets and action points.

3 COLLECTION MANAGEMENT

3.1 Current collections

The librarian is responsible for the management and development of the current collections that support the teaching, learning and research activities of the institution.

The library should have a collection development policy, which should be guided by, and be consistent with, the general principles and priorities articulated in the mission statement (see **7.1.1**).

The collection development policy should cover the acquisition and disposal of books, journals, audiovisual materials and electronic resources, and should include consideration of the following:

- the level of resource provision required in each subject area e.g. undergraduate or research
- the needs of residential and non-residential students, and distance learners e.g. in the provision of online resources

- the availability of resources elsewhere e.g. via a validating university or local public library
- the provision of student book grants e.g. with regard to the purchase of multiple copies of core texts
- the availability of free online resources

3.1.1 Books

Teaching staff have a responsibility to recommend books for the library, based on the needs of the courses they teach, their own research interests, and the agreed priorities of the library. This responsibility should be formally noted as part of the library induction of new staff. The librarian should facilitate the process by making publishers' catalogues and review journals available, for example, or by drawing attention to publishers' websites.

The librarian should also provide the opportunity for other library users to make recommendations.

However the librarian should be ultimately responsible for book purchasing decisions, and should ensure that overall spending is kept within the budget and is appropriately distributed across cost centres and / or subject areas. The librarian should also be responsible for ensuring continuity of coverage in the event of a temporary staff vacancy, for example, or in subject areas of a multidisciplinary or general nature.

For the purchase of particularly expensive items, a procedure for consultation should be established, for example through a staff group or the library committee.

Books may be purchased directly from the publisher, from a local bookshop, through a library supplier, or from an online bookseller. Some institutions have their own bookshop, in which case the library may choose this handy source of supply. Increasingly, good deals are to be found online, both for new and second hand books, and the option to purchase online should be available to the librarian. However, the following should also be taken into consideration:

- the institution may wish to support the local economy by buying locally
- significant discounts are sometimes offered to libraries when purchasing directly from a publisher
- library suppliers not only offer a discount, but also provide value-

added services, such as book processing and fund management
- there are economies of scale in using a single supplier

In general the librarian should consider the following criteria when deciding on the preferred method of book supply:

- cost (of the book)
- convenience (staff time)
- speed of delivery
- reliability
- value-added services

3.1.2 Reference collection

The librarian has a particular responsibility for the reference collection, which should cover both specialist theological reference works and also works of a more general nature. The former might include concordances, dictionaries, encyclopedias and commentaries as well as religious and denominational directories and handbooks. The latter might include a general encyclopedia, language dictionaries and an atlas.

Reference works particularly lend themselves to electronic or online delivery, and the librarian should be aware of the alternative formats in which traditional reference information can now be provided. In particular it is worth noting that most public libraries now provide free access to a wide range of online reference resources.

3.1.3 Journals

The librarian, in consultation with teaching staff, should ensure that the library subscribes to an appropriate range of print journals. With the increasing availability of online journals, it is sometimes argued that print journals are becoming redundant, but with many theological journals not yet available online, and others only available in electronic form to print subscribers, the time has not yet come to dispense with the journal collection.

However, there are good reasons for theological librarians to scrutinise their journal subscriptions closely. Online availability has contributed to a disproportionate rise in the cost of many academic titles, which tend to be priced for the university market, not for smaller institutions. Some publishers have spotted this problem, or have had it drawn to their attention, and are now offering substantial discounts to ABTAPL members who subscribe directly. The world of journal publishing is currently in a state of rapid change, and the librarian should remain alert.

The librarian should consider sourcing journals through a subscription agent. An agent offers economies of scale, with a single renewal process, a single financial transaction, and a single point of contact for claims. This can be particularly helpful in the case of subscriptions to journals published abroad. But an agent also charges commission, and this may add significantly to the cost. The librarian should consider the following criteria when deciding on the preferred method:

- cost (of the journal)
- convenience (staff time)
- reliability
- value-added services

Subject access is key to journal use. Some journals have printed indexes, but computerised searching is far more efficient and effective. Some libraries may wish to catalogue their journals to article level, with the advantage that library users will be able to search the journal and book stock together. But this is a time-intensive process. Other options include:

- Bibliographic search tools. The ATLA Religion Database has been pre-eminent in the field for many years, initially in CDROM format, now exclusively web-based. Pricing strategies have kept it just within range for some, but certainly not all, theological institutions in the UK. But other providers are emerging.
- Publishers' websites. Many publishers offer free searching of the contents pages of back issues, even where the full text is not available. Major publishers of electronic journals offer free searching to non-subscribers.
- Full-text databases. Providers offer subject-based collections of online journals, with a single search interface. Providers who link the subscription rate to the size of the institution are more likely to appeal to theological libraries.

3.1.4 Audiovisual materials

With the increasing availability of web-based resources, and the technology to create and store one's own multimedia collections, there has been a decline in the use of traditional audiovisual materials in libraries (photographs, cassettes, videos, slides etc.).

However theological libraries may possess unique collections in these formats, and adequate provision should be made for their use. They are also particularly vulnerable to deterioration, and if appropriate the librarian should consider converting the content to a digital format.

Meanwhile DVDs are rapidly replacing videos, and many books are now published with accompanying material in DVD or CD format. The librarian should formulate a policy for managing these accessories. Some will prefer the security of issuing accompanying materials separately. Others will allow them to remain with the book, in which case it is important to ensure that they are present when the book is returned from loan.

3.1.5 Electronic resources

The management of e-resources is now an integral part of the librarian's job. From CDROMs to online journals and e-books, important purchasing decisions need to be made. The librarian should be guided by the library's collection development policy, and should consult closely on these decisions with teaching staff and/or the library committee.

3.1.5.1 CDROMs

The CDROM has become a popular format for theological resources, ranging from highly sophisticated and relatively expensive software programmes such as BibleWorks to relatively cheap collections of out-of-copyright digitised texts. But the librarian should consider carefully before purchasing CDROMs for the library. For one thing, many of the resources now available in this format are also freely available online. For another, the CDROM format itself is facing an uncertain future, as products such as the ATLA Religion Database move to a web-based platform.

The librarian should also consider the issue of networking. Many theological resources on CDROM are primarily designed for individual home use, and may not legally be networked or copied. For those which may, the cost of networking is often prohibitive. Yet the demand in theological libraries, particularly those which serve a non-residential clientele, is increasingly for networked resources which are not dependent on a single PC in the library.

3.1.5.2 Online journals

Some full text online journals are freely available on the web. Others may be available through a local or validating university (see **6.2**). The librarian should assist library users in making use of these as part of the library's programme of information skills training.

Most of the major academic publishers offer online access to the full text of journals to which the library subscribes in hard copy. This access can be enabled across a campus network (by providing a range of IP addresses) or via a username and password (for off-campus use). Such online access may not come entirely free. Publishers tend to offer a range of subscription rates: print only, online only, or print and online. Some distinguish between online access which is temporary (for the duration of the subscription) and that which is guaranteed in perpetuity. Others do not include access to back runs.

Clearly it can get very complicated, both for the librarian, as administrator, and for the end user, who may be required to remember a variety of passwords, to use a range of different search interfaces, and to repeat their searches across any number of different databases.

The third option is for the library to subscribe to a subject collection of online journals. This option has clear advantages for both the librarian and the user:

- a single point of administration
- a single search interface
- only one password to remember
- a far wider range of journal titles

But the librarian should also be aware of certain caveats:

- check the list of titles for quality, relevance, and bias – not just quantity
- note that journal titles may be removed from, as well as added to, the list at any time
- check the coverage of each title – some back runs are relatively short
- check for delayed release of most recent issues – some publishers protect their subscriptions by delaying the release of the full text for up to twelve months

Subscribing to an online journals collection should be regarded as adding value to the library's journal resources, not as a substitute for a print collection (though there may be some savings at the margins). The list of titles in an online collection is determined by factors which may have little to do with the mission and priorities of an individual theological library, and will not include many important titles. There are also strong arguments in favour of continuity in a print collection, not least that online access is likely to cease with the subscription.

Students should be discouraged from over-reliance on, or over-confidence in, an online journals collection. The librarian should emphasise its shortcomings as well as its many advantages.

3.1.5.3 E-books

Electronic books, or e-books, can either be purchased individually or as part of a subject-based package of titles from a publisher. Like online journals, e-books offer the advantages of enhanced subject searching and remote access for non-residential or part-time students. They may also help meet the demand for multiple copies of core texts.

However, like online journals, e-books also have an administrative cost, and if the library decides to subscribe to a package of titles, then they may need to be catalogued. It is also likely that the degree of overlap will be relatively small between the titles offered by an individual publisher and those which the library would otherwise have purchased in hard copy. In this respect a subscription should be seen as a value-added service, not as a cost-saver, and the cost of the subscription should be weighed with this in mind.

ABTAPL has set up consortia to negotiate discounts with publishers to bring e-book packages within the range of some theological libraries.

3.1.6 Cataloguing and classification

Much has been written in recent years questioning the value of professional cataloguing and classification in the computer age. Some theological libraries have developed their own cataloguing practices and classification systems, and there may appear to be little harm in this, provided that it is effective and internally consistent. However the value of professional training in information retrieval theory should not be underestimated. Rules are the very essence of library organisation, and it is only when the rationale of published standards and systems are understood that the liberty of customisation can sometimes be taken. The librarian should therefore be responsible for all aspects of cataloguing and classification.

3.1.6.1 Cataloguing

AACR2[4] is the current internationally-recognised standard for cataloguing, and libraries maintaining a card catalogue should follow its provisions. Libraries with a computerised catalogue should continue to be guided by AACR2, even though some of its provisions, such as the distinction between Main Entry and Added Entry, may appear to have become redundant.

The standard MARC21[5] format, which facilitates the import and export of catalogue records, should be used where possible. Most library management systems now support an underlying MARC format, while presenting a more user-friendly interface to the cataloguer.

---

[4] Anglo-American Cataloguing Rules, 2nd edition. A new edition is currently in preparation under the working title Resource Description and Access (RDA).
[5] MARC21 is the current standard Machine-Readable Cataloguing format.

Adherence to these standards may not appear necessary where a library has no current need to import or export catalogue records, but there is no guarantee that this will always be the case. At some future date, it is quite possible that the library will wish to incorporate another library's collections, to contribute to a union catalogue, or to import catalogue records to save the expense of creating them. For this reason, adhering to these standards should be regarded as good practice and an investment in the future.

3.1.6.2 Subject headings

The computerised keyword search provides a cheap and helpful method of subject indexing, and some libraries rely on it to the exclusion of adding subject headings to the catalogue record. It is also true that controlled subject indexing is time-consuming and expensive. But the absence of any form of subject heading in the catalogue record undermines the effectiveness of the catalogue in delivering subject access.

Library of Congress Subject Headings (LCSH) are the standard system of subject headings used by many of the larger libraries. Purchased catalogue records are likely to include them, and at the very least they represent a useful source of keywords. At best, they can be used as the basis for controlled subject indexing, providing value-added subject access to the library's collections. The librarian should however be aware of the tendency of LCSH to reflect the American context.

3.1.6.3 Classification

A wide variety of classification schemes are used in theological libraries, ranging from the two major schemes, the Dewey Decimal Classification (DDC) and Library of Congress (LC), to schemes such as the Pettee Classification which are specifically designed for theological collections, and unconventional, home-grown schemes.

The major schemes are designed for general collections, so they can feel unwieldy in a theological library. DDC in particular has a tendency to produce long strings of numbers. Local schemes, on the other hand, often date relatively quickly and become inflexible to new developments in the subject.

Wholesale reclassification is an expensive process and is unlikely to be a viable option for a large library. A rolling programme of targeted reclassification within an existing scheme is likely to be a more practical way forward, perhaps as a summer project.

It should be remembered that classification is a means to an end and not an end in itself. First, it serves as a finding tool, guiding the user from the catalogue to the shelf. Long numbers are a potential obstacle to this, and should be avoided. Second, it facilitates browsing by grouping together material on related subjects. In this respect, a number may be completely wrong, but it is rarely perfectly right, either. It is not worth agonizing over.

It should be added that no two libraries use the same classification scheme in exactly the same way. There is always an element of in-house adaptation or interpretation. This has implications both for union catalogues and for library mergers.

3.1.7 Labelling

Classification is only effective if it is accompanied by clear labelling. A legible font and size should be used[6], preferably black on white. The label should be robust, but also removable in order to facilitate correction or reclassification at a later date.

3.1.8 Weeding

An important part of the maintenance of any collection is the weeding of little-used or out-of-date stock, both for reasons of space and to keep the collection fresh and relevant. The key factor in the quality of a library's collections is not the number of books and journals, but their relevance to the needs of users. In the context of weeding, it is particularly important to take into consideration the possible relevance of material for research.

The librarian is responsible for establishing weeding criteria, which should be consistent with the library's collection development policy. The criteria should be agreed with the library committee, and should be publicly available. Withdrawing stock can sometimes be contentious, and it is important that the

---

[6] For helpful advice on font style, see the British Dyslexia Association's style guide at http://www.bdadyslexia.org.uk/extra352.html (accessed 30.11.07)

process is open and accountable. Criteria might include:

- currency
- usage
- relevance to current teaching or research
- the availability of a more recent edition of a book
- multiple copies of texts no longer on reading lists

Teaching staff, with their awareness of current trends within their subject area, should be closely consulted for their advice on relevance and currency. Automated library management systems now make it easier to monitor patterns of usage.

Little-used material which may nevertheless be of historical or research value should be moved to an alternative location. Compact shelving is ideal for this purpose, and for a library with space constraints is likely to be a cheaper alternative to building an extension.

3.1.9 Disposal

Material which is no longer required should be disposed of. Unlike rare books and archives, books weeded from current collections are unlikely to be of significant value, and it may not be cost effective to produce detailed lists for prospective buyers unless there is a simple way of doing so. Nevertheless it is worth inviting second-hand dealers specialising in the subject to view them. There is rarely any money in weeded journals, but these are more easily listed, and may be offered either to other theological libraries or to cooperative schemes.

Another option is to sell off weeded stock to students. Regular book sales can help to supplement the library budget, though the librarian should ensure that there is no scope for confusion between books which are for sale and books which are not!

A third option is to offer weeded stock to a charity such as Book Aid, which makes withdrawn library books available to libraries in the developing world. Responsible organisations apply their own rigorous selection criteria to the books they receive, and will simply dispose of some of them. But those which are of use will find a good home.

Weeding and disposing of library stock in a responsible manner is a necessary but time-consuming task. The librarian should balance any income which may be generated against the costs of the process itself.

3.1.10 Stock check

No security system is a complete safeguard against loss (see **7.3**), and the library's stock should therefore be checked from time to time. Borrowing may need to be suspended for a complete stock check, but the summer vacation could be an appropriate time for this, especially if volunteer labour can be recruited to assist with the task. Alternatively, a limited stock check could focus on core texts, or a rolling programme could be set up so that the whole stock is checked over, say, a five year period.

Many library management systems now provide a stock check module, or the shelves may be manually checked against printed lists.

The main reason for checking is to produce hard evidence of the loss of stock. This is essential for a serious debate about library security measures. The numbers are usually much higher than most people would imagine, and the cost of security needs to be set against the cost of replacing lost books. But a stock check also has the added benefit of tidying up the library, and relocating books which have been lost through mis-shelving during the course of the year.

3.2 Rare books and archives

Besides the current collections which support teaching and research, some theological libraries also hold collections of rare books and archives, and it is important to understand the rationale for such collections. They may represent a significant research resource, consistent with the library's mission; they may relate closely to the historic identity of the institution; or they may commemorate benefactors or historically significant figures. Alternatively, they may have ended up there more by accident than by design. The value and significance of the collection needs to be carefully assessed.

The institution should be aware of the responsibilities entailed in maintaining and conserving such collections, and should provide an appropriate environment for them[7]. Archives in particular have special needs, but are prone to neglect. One

---

[7] British Standard BS5454:2000 includes recommendations for the storage of rare books and archives

38

common problem is an assumption that archives merely require storage space, and not space for consultation or listing work. In fact archives require substantially more workspace than printed books, and they require more specialised workspace. A second common assumption is that archives are very much like books, and can be left to the librarian to deal with. In fact archives administration is quite different from library administration, and requires special skills that many librarians have not been trained in. It is also often assumed that archives have no special security requirements. In fact many archives, particularly modern archives, contain sensitive materials that may not be published. Free access to archives cannot be given in the same way as it can to books.

Rare books collections also incur management costs which are often underestimated, particularly with regard to conservation. Neglect is a slow but inevitable form of destruction. Another consideration is the increasing availability of out-of-copyright texts in digitised form. 'Rare' books may not now be so rare.

For these reasons the institution should either recognise and accept its responsibilities (financial and moral) for maintaining the collections within the library, or it should seriously consider whether they would not be better preserved and housed elsewhere.

3.2.1 Maintaining collections

Where an institution possesses substantial archives and wishes to retain them, it should ideally employ a qualified archivist to look after them. At the very least it should seek the advice of the professional bodies and national agencies that provide advice and guidance on the treatment and conservation of archives. Significant archives are normally regarded as part of the nation's heritage, and archive collections can therefore expect much more help in terms of free advice and nationally funded assistance. The MLA Partnership's Designation Scheme[8] is one such programme.

In the management of rare books and smaller archive collections, the institution should support the librarian in the following ways:

---

[8] The MLA Partnership is a government agency for museums, libraries, and archives. For details of the Designation Scheme see http://www.mla.gov.uk/website/programmes/designation (accessed 15.11.07)

3.2.1.1 Conservation

The institution should provide a regular budget for a programme of conservation and repairs to books and documents. Expenditure may also be required for physical alterations to the environment in which the books and documents are kept, to minimise their vulnerability to theft and vandalism, and to damage from direct sunlight, high humidity, flooding, fire, mould, and insects.

Funding may also be required to retain the services of a specialist conservation consultant to advise on storage conditions, the development of a disaster plan, and priorities for conservation and repair work.

The librarian should be encouraged to gain further knowledge and experience in the field of conservation.

3.2.1.2 Accessibility and security

Provision should be made for the listing or cataloguing of the collections so that they are accessible to researchers. Archives and rare books have particular and distinctive cataloguing requirements, which are likely to require specialist training, and the institution should be prepared to fund this.

Security should be a particular concern in the housing and storage of rare books and archives, and provision should be made for supervised consultation of the collection.

The library should have a written policy on its special collections, governing conservation, security, and access.

3.2.2 Disposing of collections

Where a decision is made to dispose of collections of rare books or archives, the institution should consider very carefully – from both a moral and a public relations point of view – where they should go. The responsibility for rare books and archives does not cease with the decision to dispose of them.

A collection of books or archives that has historical significance *as a collection* should not be dispersed, but should so far as is possible be housed with related collections in an institution that is equipped to conserve, maintain and make accessible the collection without disturbing its integrity. This may, for example, be a local university library, or a specialist research library.

In general, sale of individual items is bad public relations. If absolutely necessary, it must be handled as carefully and as responsibly as possible. The institution should check that it has the right to sell. If appropriate, it should consult with donors of the items or their heirs, and seek their agreement. In the case of scarce items, it should approach national deposit and research libraries and suggest a direct purchase before placing them on the open market.

It is also recommended that one of the leading auction houses, such as Christies or Sothebys, is consulted to advise on the market value of the collection or of individual items within it.

3.3 Donations

Theological libraries are often offered donations, ranging from individual items, to the collections of deceased or retired clergy, to institutional or personal archives. Donations, while always well intentioned, should be treated strictly on their merits, and the same criteria should be applied to their acquisition as to that of other library resources. The librarian should make clear that donated materials are never 'free' – there are always costs associated with their management.

The librarian should discourage donations which come with strings attached. Donors should be asked to agree that their donation may be deployed at the librarian's discretion. This may mean adding books to stock; it may mean selling them and adding the proceeds to library funds; or it may mean advising the donor of a more appropriate repository.

If the donation has a wider significance for the institution, then the librarian should advise on the costs and other implications of receiving it.

4 INFORMATION TECHNOLOGY

Developments in information technology represent the single biggest change affecting libraries in the past twenty years. In response librarians have had to acquire their own IT skills, and also to work closely with specialist IT staff. Without these skills and this cooperation, librarians cannot hope to meet the needs of their users in the twenty first century.

Within higher and further education a common response has been to converge library and IT services within a single department, often under the heading of 'information services'. With a converged service it is easier to agree priorities and work to common goals. But it can be challenging bringing together the very different cultures and working styles to be found within the library and IT sectors. Working together is not always easy.

Within theological institutions it is rare to find a converged service. Instead a variety of solutions have evolved, such as contracting out IT support, or making use of the expertise of an existing staff member (who may or may not be the librarian), or relying on voluntary support. IT costs can be a serious drain for small institutions, but the costs of not investing in IT can be even higher. Institutions should pay particular attention to the management of IT-related information, and should be wary of relying too heavily on short-term volunteers such as students who are likely to take the information away with them when they leave.

For most institutions, a formal and accountable structure for managing and prioritising IT needs is strongly recommended. This might include the appointment of an IT director, setting up an IT committee, and developing an institutional IT strategy. In the absence of such a structure, the librarian will have to work hard at building up collaborative relationships and advocating the library's needs to ensure that they are not neglected.

There are two areas in which IT support is particularly important for the library:

- the library management system
- the e-learning environment

4.1 The library management system

Most theological institutions now have a computerised catalogue, and many have moved to a fully automated system for some or all of circulation, acquisitions and serials management. The librarian is responsible for selecting and managing the library management system, but should seek specialist advice on hardware and networking requirements.

If the library does not already have a computerised system, then the librarian should consider the advantages and disadvantages of purchasing one. Not all libraries need a library management system. For some libraries, with small budgets, low levels of use, and a small, locally-based clientele, it will not be cost-effective. But most libraries will experience significant benefits from automating some or all of their processes. The advantages to the library user include enhanced searching of the catalogue, and remote access to the catalogue and loans information. The advantages to the librarian include more efficient use of staff time, and enhanced management information. But the institution should also be aware of the additional workload, ongoing costs, and the potential for technical problems.

Once a decision has been made to purchase a library management system for the first time, or to migrate to a new system, then the librarian should consider some or all of the following during the selection process:

- Be clear about what you want from your system, and what the system can deliver. Make a list of essential and desirable functionality.
- Shop around. See the various systems in action. CILIP runs regular supplier demonstrations, where you can see different systems side by side, but there is no substitute for visiting a library which runs the system.
- Talk to existing clients, especially to theological librarians, whose requirements are likely to be similar to your own. Ask about the quality of support provided by the supplier. Find out about user groups.
- Find out about the supplier's future plans. In a rapidly changing environment, is the system stagnating or developing?
- Check the compatibility of the system with your institution's existing software and hardware infrastructure. Anticipate additional costs.

Once a library management system has been purchased, the librarian is responsible for managing it. In the past it has been possible to manage a small system exclusively from the library, and it has been reasonable to expect the librarian to possess the skills to do so. But as systems have become more complex, there has been a corresponding need for a more sophisticated infrastructure and a higher level of IT skills. Some aspects of systems management have thus moved from the domain of the librarian (both physical and managerial) to the domain of the IT specialist. The librarian should continue to have exclusive responsibility for the library applications software, but may not have unrestricted access to the server.

In the modern environment maintenance and problem-solving can sometimes necessitate a rather complicated three-way conversation between the librarian, the system supplier and IT support staff. The institution should support the librarian in ensuring that structures are in place to facilitate this.

4.2 The e-learning environment

IT support is also critical to the institution's e-learning environment. Most institutions support a local area network, and some are beginning to experiment with wireless networks. But networked computing facilities should continue to be provided in the library, enabling the library service to provide integrated access to a full range of print and electronic resources. This is the essence of the modern 'hybrid' library.

The librarian should be responsible for supporting the use of the computers in the library, not only providing support for library resources but also technical trouble-shooting. Training should be provided, and a procedure should be in place for referring more complex problems to an IT specialist.

The librarian should also be responsible for maintaining and developing the library website. A website is now a vital tool for any institution, providing information to current members and acting as a shop window to the wider world. It is worth investing in the skills of a web design consultant to create the initial design and house style. But once a website has been established, the librarian should be able to create and edit library web pages to serve as a single reference point to library services and to provide a link to the library catalogue. New software applications are making web authoring more accessible.

Within higher and further education, virtual learning environments (VLEs) integrate library services (such as the library catalogue and online journals) with web-based learning resources and interactive discussion facilities. Some theological institutions are beginning to incorporate some of the features of these systems into their own in-house learning environments. An institutional approach should be taken to the development of virtual learning environments, involving teaching staff, the librarian, and IT support. If the process is not managed at an institutional level, the virtual learning environment is likely to develop in a piecemeal way, with duplication of effort, and confusion for students.

5 INFORMATION LITERACY

Information literacy is a relatively new concept, and encompasses traditional library user education as well as modern information skills, IT skills, and study skills. It has emerged largely in response to developments in information technology. Far more information is now available in a wider range of formats, and more highly developed skills are required not only to access the information, but also to manage, evaluate, and use it. One of the symptoms of the challenge is the plethora of terms used to describe the skills required. Information literacy is just one of the terms now in common currency, but its general acceptance within the library world has been recognised by the adoption of a formal definition by CILIP [9].

Discussions of information literacy have raised a variety of questions: should institutions run a separate, generic information literacy programme, or should the teaching of information literacy be subject-related and embedded in the curriculum? If separate, should the programme be compulsory or optional? If

---

[9]
See http://www.cilip.org.uk/policyadvocacy/informationliteracy/ (accessed 19.11.07)

compulsory, should it be credit-bearing? But perhaps the most important question is who should take the lead on information literacy within the institution. Responsibility is unlikely to fall within the remit of a single department. Rather, library, IT, and teaching staff all have a contribution to make in the programme. The evidence suggests that information literacy programmes are most successful when they are directed at a senior level, either in the form of an individual, such as a director of studies, or of a committee, such as a teaching committee, with authority across the curriculum. However, the librarian should have an important role, not only in delivering a substantial part of an information literacy programme, but also in promoting the concept of information literacy within the institution.

5.1 Information literacy programme

An information literacy programme in a theological institution might include some or all of the following:

- how to use the library catalogue
- how to use the journal literature
- how to use the internet for theological resources

- how to search full text electronic databases
- how to use CDROMs e.g. BibleWorks

- how to use word processing, spreadsheet and presentation software
- how to use email

- how to identify one's own learning style
- how to read and make notes
- how to structure an essay
- how to cite references

- how to identify and evaluate information sources
- how to gather and store information (including the use of bibliographic software)

- intellectual property and copyright
- plagiarism

5.2 Library induction

There is no substitute for library induction, which is in essence a basic introduction to services, resources, and the library building. It enables experienced students to use the library, and it gives less experienced students the confidence to make a start and to know where to come for further help. It also enables the librarian to establish the ethos of the library service.

A personal library induction, led by a member of the library staff, with attendance compulsory, at the beginning of the course of study, is always the ideal. But some theological libraries are now beginning to develop 'virtual' library induction (an interactive online guide), following the trend set by higher and further education libraries to cope with rising student numbers. This is certainly worth exploring, not just because overall student numbers are rising in some institutions, but also because the diverse range of pathways being pursued by theological students is likely to create a demand for library induction at different times. A great deal of staff time can be spent offering induction to small groups, or even individuals, throughout the course of the year. 'Virtual' library induction offers students the opportunity to participate at a time of their own choosing. But even the best programme will lack the advantages of the personal touch.

5.3 User education

Library user education should include the provision of written guides to services, preferably available both in print and online, as well as training sessions on particular services, such as how to use the catalogue, print and online journals, and CDROMs. It may be appropriate to offer some of these sessions at a later stage in the first term. Students are unlikely to be at their most receptive during the first week. Online tutorials may also be developed to enable students to participate in their own time, or as a refresher, and students should also be referred to the Intute interactive tutorial designed to help higher education students use the internet for religious studies and theology [10].

The librarian should continue to provide support for the use of library resources as required, but when demand is high and time is short, it may be appropriate to schedule group training to meet the need.

---

[10] See http://www.vts.intute.ac.uk/he/tutorial/religion (accessed 19.11.07)

6 LIBRARY COOPERATION

Librarians usually seek to cooperate. In part this is in recognition of the costs to be saved by sharing resources. But there is also a strong ethos of mutual support within the profession, and a sense of being involved together in a larger enterprise of public service. This is particularly true of the network of theological libraries which constitutes the ABTAPL membership[11].

Library cooperation has been particularly evident in the systems of interlibrary loans, both formal and informal, which have developed over many years. But the shift towards electronic resource provision is beginning to have significant implications for relationships between libraries. In particular it is exposing the essential inequality of many library relationships. For small theological libraries, the potential benefits of resource sharing are greater, but the relationships are more complex, and often beyond the scope of simple good will between librarians.

---

[11] See http://www.abtapl.org.uk/ for information about joining the ABTAPL Discussion List

6.1 Interlibrary loans

A range of options are available to the librarian when a request is made for an item which is not in stock or available online. The first option is to buy it. The same criteria should be applied to the purchase of requested items as to other recommendations. Sometimes it is cheaper to buy a book than to borrow it.

The second option is to refer the user to a local library which stocks the item. This may include the local public library, or a local university library with which an access or borrowing arrangement is in place.

Only when these options have been discounted should the librarian consider obtaining the item by interlibrary loan:

- The British Library loans books and supplies copies of journal articles to higher education institutions at a discounted rate. The librarian must decide whether to pass on the whole cost to the user, or to subsidise it from library funds.

- ABTAPL libraries which are free to do so cooperate in an informal interlibrary loans network, loaning books at their discretion and supplying copies of journal articles more cheaply than the British Library.

- The public library service offers a heavily-subsidised interlibrary loans service (the exact charge varies between local authorities), but it tends to be slower than the service offered by the British Library.

The library should have a clearly defined interlibrary loans policy, stating which options are available, and who pays. The librarian should take into consideration local circumstances (e.g. access to good local libraries), staff time, and the library budget.

6.2 Electronic resources

Many theological libraries have some sort of relationship with a university library. Traditionally this has involved a reciprocal access or borrowing arrangement agreed between library staff, though the usefulness of such an arrangement will depend largely on the degree of overlap between the courses on offer at the respective institutions. The relationship may be linked to the role of the university in validating the 'affiliated' institution's courses, and in recent years such relationships have become more formal, based less on the professional good will of librarians, and more on the requirements of the Higher Education Funding Council. Universities have been keen to bolster their notional student numbers in order to attract more funding, and in return for including affiliated students in the figures they have been obliged to offer them library services.

The level of service offered to the students of affiliated institutions varies considerably. Some are entitled to access to the university's electronic resources, while others are not. The picture was clearer when electronic resources were accessible to walk-in users. But the shift from CDROM to web-based services, together with the emergence of highly complex licensing arrangements and password-controlled access, has sometimes led to the exclusion of affiliated students. The variety of institutional relationships, and differences in the wording of licences, make it something of a grey area in legal and administrative terms, and universities have been understandably cautious in their approach.

Shared access to electronic resources is a big issue for theological libraries, with major implications for their own collection development strategy. The librarian should be cautious about relying too heavily on access to resources which may be withdrawn at a later date, but the potential for cost savings on the one hand and for enhancing the library service on the other is considerable. Public library authorities are also beginning to make some major academic resources available online to members free of charge.

It is worth emphasising that the librarian should encourage library users to take up the opportunities offered by local academic and public libraries, not only to make use of the resources available, but also as part of their preparation for lifelong learning.

6.3 Expertise

Shared resources are not the only way in which library cooperation is important for the theological librarian. In many other ways bigger institutions can offer expertise and support which is not available in a smaller institution. University libraries and public library authorities employ specialists in areas ranging from rare books, special collections and conservation, to copyright and interlibrary loans. The theological librarian should make every effort to cultivate these relationships and draw upon this expertise.

7 LIBRARY MANAGEMENT

Library management encompasses a wide range of responsibilities, from establishing a planning and monitoring framework to managing individual aspects of the library service.

7.1 Planning and monitoring

The librarian is responsible for ensuring that a framework is in place for planning and monitoring the library service. The framework should include:

- a mission statement (or equivalent)
- annual reporting
- performance monitoring

7.1.1 Mission statement

The purpose of a mission statement is to set the direction for the library service, and it should be the reference point for all other library policy statements. Where appropriate, it should be guided by, and be consistent with, the institution's mission and ethos. It should give a broad indication of who the library is for, what its purpose is, what its priorities are, and how it aims to achieve them. The mission statement should be discussed with the library committee, be approved by the Academic Board, and be publicly available.

7.1.2 Annual reporting

The librarian should write an annual report, which should include a review of the past year and set the agenda for the year ahead. The annual report is an important tool for internal planning and for external communication. It should be written in consultation with the librarian's line manager and the library committee, and it should be circulated to the Academic Board and the institution's governing body. It has an important role in raising the profile of the library within the institution.

7.1.3 Performance monitoring

The librarian is responsible for monitoring the performance of the library service through the use of statistical indicators and user feedback.

A wide range of statistics can be monitored, from the number of books on the shelves to the number of study spaces per user. But statistics on their own are simply raw data. They need to be used with discernment if they are to be useful indicators of performance and not just measures of quantity. For the librarian, statistics can be useful in the following ways:

- to inform library planning e.g. low level of use of a particular service may suggest that the service needs to be more widely promoted
- to support the librarian's case within the institution e.g. high demand may suggest that more money needs to be spent on a particular service
- to measure progress towards a particular objective e.g. monitoring online journal use by distance learners
- for benchmarking – it may not always be appropriate to make comparisons with other libraries, but sometimes it is helpful to be aware of national standards or statistics from other theological libraries
- for apportioning costs – the librarian may be required to apportion library costs to cost centres, such as academic departments, and a range of usage statistics can be helpful in this respect

Library management systems now make it much easier to monitor many aspects of library usage. Commercial databases are also able to provide usage statistics, and the more sophisticated swipe card systems can provide data on users entering the library. But in other areas, such as enquiry work or the use of non-loanable materials, the librarian should devise ad hoc systems for statistical monitoring.

Feedback from library users is another useful indicator of performance. The librarian should ensure that formal mechanisms are in place to facilitate this (e.g. feedback forms in the library, user representation on the library committee, an annual survey) and should also encourage informal feedback (e.g. by email). But feedback received from users should not dictate the development of library policy. There is often a discrepancy between perception and reality, and users' perceptions of the library service may suggest a need for better communication rather than a change in policy.

7.2 Financial management

The librarian is responsible for advising the institution on the financial needs of the library, and for monitoring the library budget.

The budget should cover library resources, office expenses, and conservation and binding (if appropriate). Depending on the model preferred by the institution, it may also cover overheads, IT costs, equipment and furniture, staff salaries, and training and professional development.

The budget should be allocated on an annual basis, and should be sufficient to enable the library to fulfil its aims and objectives.

The monitoring of spending on library resources is likely to be the most complex part of the process. Depending on the model preferred by the institution, the librarian may be required to apportion costs to cost centres.

7.3 Library security

The librarian should consider seriously the issues around library security. Some theological libraries hold rare and valuable materials which may be the target of deliberate theft, and measures should be taken to protect these. Many libraries have also invested heavily in IT equipment, for which special security provision should be made. But the loss of library materials is more likely to be the result of carelessness, negligence, or an inappropriate attitude to library property and the wider user community. One response the librarian should consider is to take steps to inculcate a greater sense of responsibility in library use, possibly as part of the induction programme.

Another key issue is whether to limit library access to times when the library is staffed. In smaller libraries this would be very restrictive, and even in larger libraries the benefits of 24-hour access would be denied. In terms of staff costs and extended opening hours, there are considerable advantages in running a library on the basis of trust.

A swipe card entry system (or equivalent) can place some restrictions on access without impinging upon the convenience of the majority of users. Alternatively, some libraries have invested in expensive electronic security systems, but even these are only effective if someone is available to monitor them.

No system is a complete safeguard against loss, and the librarian should weigh up the respective costs of accessibility and security.

7.4 The library building

Theological library buildings come in all shapes and sizes. Some were not originally designed to be libraries. Others are ill-suited to the demands of a modern library with its associated IT requirements, extended study space and growing collections. In the first instance it is the responsibility of the librarian to make best use of what is given, providing appropriate signs and guides to help users find their way round. Signs should be eye-catching and attractive. Shabby notices create a poor impression.

The opportunity to build a new library or to extend an existing one will almost certainly depend on external factors, such as a timely bequest. But if the existing library building is clearly unfit for purpose, or is likely to become so in the near future, then the librarian should be prepared to say so, and to make the case for a major building project if the funds become available.

In the event of a major building project the librarian should ensure that the architect and the project manager are fully appraised of the library's needs. A library building has particular requirements – such as a stable environment – which may not be apparent to other professionals, and the librarian should be closely involved at every stage, from the initial design, through each draft of the architect's plan, to the detailed implementation. It is recommended that the opportunity is taken to visit other new library buildings at an early stage of the process, to learn the lessons where things went wrong, and to draw inspiration from what went right.

7.5 Disaster planning

Disaster planning sounds rather dramatic, and it is sometimes tempting to assume that "it will never happen to us". But serious disasters – in the form of fire or flood – do happen, and it is the responsibility of the librarian to minimise the risk and to be prepared for the event. Even a small amount of water can do a surprising amount of damage to library materials. Disaster planning should encompass small "disasters" as well as major ones.

The library should have a written policy, covering disaster prevention and preparedness, and a disaster plan detailing actions in response to an event. Disasters do not always strike during office hours, and for this reason it is essential that the disaster plan is available in the library and familiar to other key members of staff. It should include details such as the location of keys and emergency equipment, and contact information for emergency services. A rapid response is essential if the damage is to be kept to a minimum, and for this reason it is recommended that a service agreement is taken out with a specialist library salvage company which guarantees priority assistance. Local libraries may also agree to help each other if the need arises.

The disaster plan should be reviewed regularly to ensure that the details are up to date. The institution should be aware of the potential cost of a major disaster, and should ensure that appropriate insurance cover is in place.

7.5.1 Valuation and insurance

Valuation of a library for insurance purposes is problematic. It is clearly unrealistic to attempt to calculate and maintain a 'real' stock valuation on an individual book-by-book basis. It is much easier to calculate a notional valuation based on current average book prices (multiplied by the number of items in the collection), but in either case the likely insurance premium for direct replacement cover will probably be unaffordable. The next best option is to take out as much total loss cover as possible. If the worst happens, the insurers would then write off the library stock completely, and pay out a sum designed to enable the purchase of a new core stock to begin rebuilding the collection from scratch. If a library holds any particularly valuable items, consideration should obviously be given to insuring these separately, in which case expert advice should be sought.

7.6 External use

There is inevitably considerable variation in current practice in relation to external use of theological libraries. Some libraries have adopted a relatively exclusive policy, offering external membership only to specific groups, such as local clergy, or members of institutions with whom there is a reciprocal arrangement. Others take a more inclusive approach, offering membership to anyone who is prepared to pay. Some libraries offer reference use only, while others offer a full range of services, including borrowing rights and access to electronic resources. There is also variation in the ways in which libraries define their external members, in the fees they charge, and in the concessions they offer.

A number of recent developments are likely to affect the demand for external use of theological libraries:

- library websites, and online catalogues in particular, are making it easier for people to find out about libraries and to locate resources
- demand from students of other institutions is growing, partly because of the growing popularity of distance learning, and partly because some institutions are unable or unwilling to resource their own courses
- the growing interest in theological education and training, including training for lay ministry and pre- and post-ordination training

In the light of this growing demand and variation in practice, it is important that the library has a clear policy on external membership. The policy should indicate who is entitled to external membership, how much it costs, what the entitlement includes, and when access to the library is permitted. It should be consistent with the library's mission statement (see **7.1.1**), balancing the desire to be hospitable and to facilitate the use of the library's resources with the need for security and to safeguard the interests of the institution's own staff and students. In particular the librarian should use available management information (such as the number of visits or loans) to establish the net cost of external use, both in terms of staff time and in terms of its impact on other library users.

Some of the issues relating to external use of the library, such as relationships with other institutions or church bodies, are institutional in nature. It is therefore appropriate to consult with institutional representatives (for example, the library committee). The policy should be publicly available, so that external people know what their entitlements are and understand the rationale behind them.

7.7 Promotion and advocacy

Promoting the library service and advocating its cause are related and sometimes neglected aspects of library management. If the library is well funded and well used, then the need for promotion and advocacy may not be apparent. But as the modern library becomes increasingly dependent on institutional support and ever more expensive to run, it is important that the librarian is constantly seeking to raise the library's profile and is able to demonstrate its value.

Raising and maintaining the library's profile is an important aspect of both promotion and advocacy. Library guides and leaflets, induction and information skills training, and displays and exhibitions have an important part to play in raising the profile of library services and resources. But articles in newsletters, a prominent web presence, and personal advocacy at meetings are just as likely to keep the library 'brand' visible. Above all informal opportunities to nurture relationships with staff, students, governors, and visitors should not be neglected.

From time to time it may also become necessary to demonstrate the value of the library. When an institution's finances are limited, for example, departments may find themselves competing with each other for funds, or a governing body may see the internet as a cheap alternative to a traditional library with the result that the library becomes an easy target for cuts. In these circumstances the librarian should emphasise the following points:

- the personal and professional contribution of library staff in all aspects of the library service

- the specific focus on the institution's teaching, learning and research needs and the use of rigorous selection criteria in the purchase of library resources
- the contribution of the library to the accreditation of the institution
- the marketing potential of the library in the recruitment of staff and students
- the risks of overdependence on other libraries
- the risks of overdependence on electronic media in general and freely available online resources and search engines in particular

7.8 Photocopying, scanning, and copyright

The provision of photocopying and scanning facilities in the library represents a valuable service and a potential source of income, although the cost of regular maintenance, consumables such as toner, and staff time spent on trouble shooting should also be taken into consideration.

The institution has a legal responsibility to take reasonable measures to ensure that copyright law, in the form of the 1988 Copyright Act and its supplementary legislation, is not abused on its premises[12]. The librarian should therefore ensure that a copyright notice is prominently displayed in the vicinity of self-service equipment, and requests for copies should be accompanied by a signed copyright declaration form.

The Copyright Licensing Agency (CLA)[13] licenses higher education institutions to make multiple copies for students in a class. The current licence covers both photocopies and digital copies. The librarian may be asked to advise on issues relating to copyright in general or the CLA licence in particular. The CLA are always happy to advise, and specialist colleagues in the university sector may also be able to help.

7.9 Other legal responsibilities

The librarian may also have some responsibility for the implementation of health and safety, equal opportunities, and data protection legislation in the context of institutional policy on these issues.

---

[12] For further information see: Graham P. Cornish. *Copyright: interpreting the law for libraries, archives and information services* (4th ed.). London: Facet Publishing, 2004.
[13] See http://www.cla.co.uk/ (accessed 19.11.07)

7.9.1 Health and safety

The librarian should be aware of the health and safety policy of the institution, and relevant health and safety legislation. Librarians have a duty of care both to their staff and to themselves, and should be familiar with the Workplace (Health, Safety and Welfare) Regulations 1992. A helpful article on health and safety law and the librarian appeared in the ABTAPL *Bulletin* in 2005[14].

7.9.2 Equal opportunities

The librarian should be aware of the equal opportunities policy of the institution, and relevant equal opportunities legislation. For example, the Disability Discrimination Act 1995 makes it unlawful for any student to be treated differently from other students on grounds of their disability. The Museums, Libraries and Archives Council (MLA) provides useful advice and suggestions that will help to ensure that the library and its

---

[14] Marion Gibson. "Health and safety at work – 'The law and the librarian revisited'", *Bulletin of ABTAPL* Vol.12 No.3 November 2005, p.19-27.

resources are both accessible and compliant[15].

7.9.3 Data protection

The management of library systems requires the gathering and storing of personal data relating to library users. The librarian should be aware of the provisions of the Data Protection Act 1998. More information is available via the website of the Information Commissioner's Office[16].

---

[15] See http://www.mla.gov.uk/website/policy/Diversity/People_With_Disabilities/ (accessed 19.11.07)

[16] See http://www.ico.gov.uk/what_we_cover/data_protection.aspx (accessed 30.11.07)

8 CONCLUSION

In this booklet the authors have set out to provide broad guidelines for theological libraries which it is hoped will be of practical use to both librarians and their employers. They make no claim to be comprehensive, and further reading is recommended for more information on particular topics[17].

The authors have avoided where possible making reference to specific companies or products. It is hoped that the focus on general principles will enable the guidelines to remain relevant and useful into the future. Nevertheless we can be sure that developments in technology in particular will continue to drive change in theological librarianship as elsewhere. The challenge for the librarian is to keep up to date with these developments and to embrace the opportunities which they represent. The challenge for the parent institution is to be willing to invest in the future, and to support the library in this rapidly changing environment.

---

[17] In particular it is recommended that the guidelines produced for the Colleges of Further and Higher Education Group (CoFHE) of CILIP are consulted: Andrew Eynon (ed.) *Guidelines for colleges: recommendations for learning resources* (7th ed.). London: Facet Publishing, 2005.